Happy Mother's Day
to the best
Nana!

May your Mother's Day make you
smile and your heart blossom.

When a child is born so is a Nana!

Nana's hold our tiny hands for just a while,

but our hearts forever.

Nana's hold our tiny hands for just a while,

but our hearts forever.

A Nana always has love to give

And time to spare.

A Nana is always there.

We love you to the moon and back!

We love you to the moon and back!

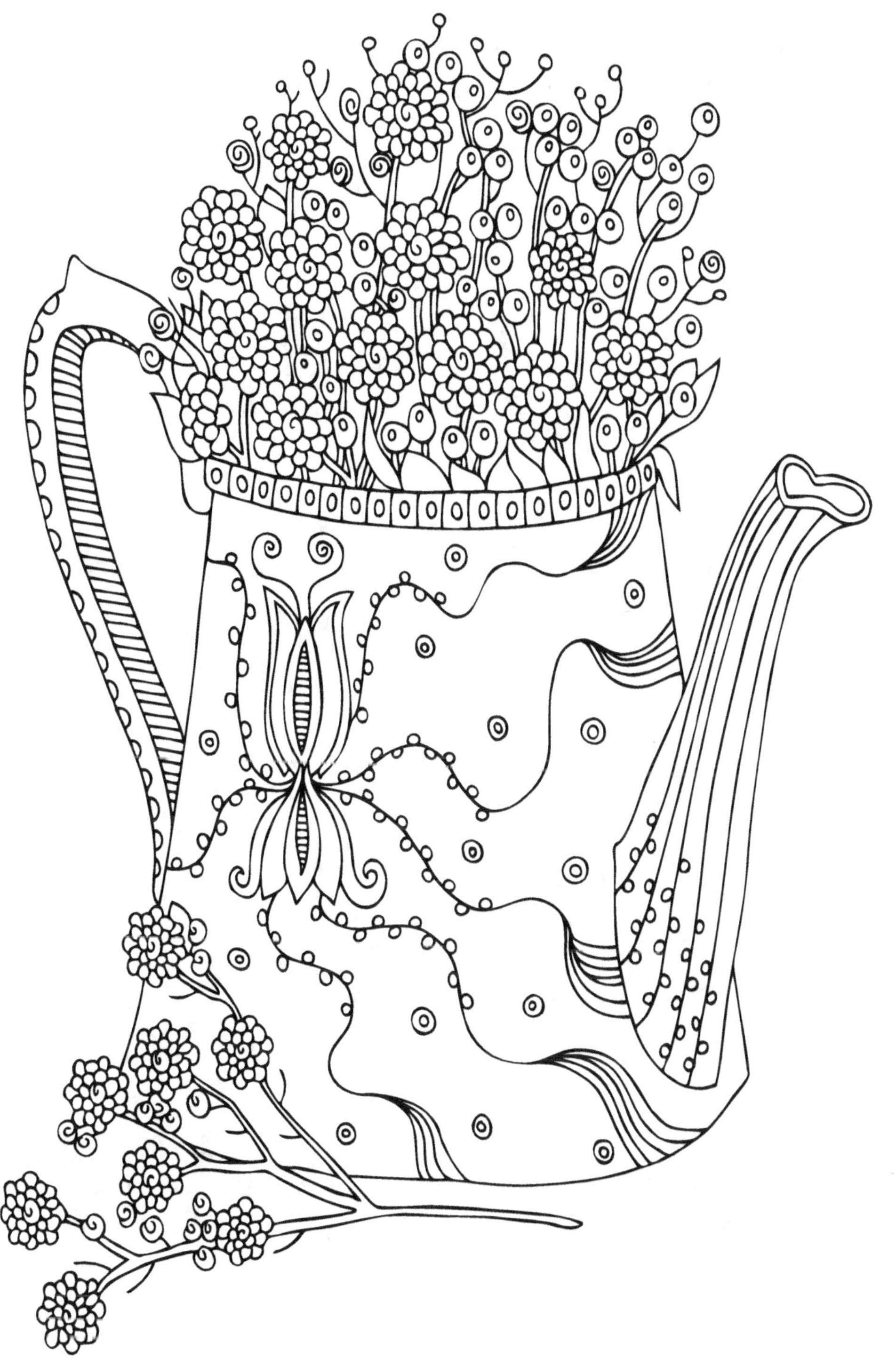

May your Mother's Day be as
bright and beautiful as you are!

You are always in my heart.

LOVE

I love you from the top of my head
To the tips of my toes!

Every day is special with a Nana like you.

Every day is special with a Nana like you.

Nanas are moms with lots of frosting!

Nanas are moms with lots of frosting!

A Nana's love feels like nobody else's.

You deserve to have all of your
dreams come true.

You deserve to have all of your
dreams come true.

flowers for your special day!

Wishing you a day that is
just like you want it to be!

Happy Mother's Day to the best
Nana!

(Coloring Card)

Copyright 2018

Sending you love, hugs, and kisses on
Mother's Day!

from